W9-BYI-389

ArethaFranklin

text   **James T. Olson**
illustrations   **John Keely**
design concept   **Mark Landkamer**

published by   **Creative Education**
    Mankato, Minnesota

Published by Creative Educational Society, Inc.,
123 South Broad Street, Mankato, Minnesota 56001
Copyright © 1975 by Creative Educational Society, Inc. International
copyrights reserved in all countries.
No part of this book may be reproduced in any form without written permission
from the publisher. Printed in the United States.
Distributed by Childrens Press, 1224 West Van Buren Street, Chicago, Illinois 60607
Library of Congress Number: 74-14672   ISBN: 74-14672

Library of Congress Cataloging in Publication Data
Olson, James T   Aretha Franklin.
SUMMARY: A brief biography emphasizing the career of Aretha Franklin.
1. Franklin, Aretha—Juvenile lit.
[1. Franklin, Aretha. 2. Singers, American]
I. Keely, John, illus. II. Title.
ML3930.F6805   784'.092'4 [B] [92]   74-14672
ISBN 0-87191-390-9

Aretha Franklin

The crowd was restless. They had just finished hearing a female rock group, Sweethearts of Soul. Now they were ready for the main event; they were ready for Aretha Franklin.

Then onto the stage of Harlem's Apollo Theater stepped Aretha. As she moved through the blinding, beaming spotlights, the announcer said: "Once in a great while comes a moment really super in music. This is such a moment. Here's Sister Soul."

The crowd went wild. A group of young people tried to get onto the stage. In the balcony, couples started dancing without music. At the center of the stage stood Aretha in a glittering silver dress. She walked over to the mike. She sang, "Yeh, deh, yeh, deh, deh, deh, deh, there is a rose in Spanish Harlem . . ."

Aretha leaned back and let that audience hear her rich, melodic voice pour forth songs. She knew those songs well. Some she had written herself, some she had sung from the time she was eight years old, and some had been especially written for her; but she knew them all well. The audience yelped explosively as she moved from one song to another.

The audience's roar increased when Sister Superstar moved over to the grand piano and started to accompany herself in four-four time. As the audience went mad, Aretha racked out song after song, rising above the noise and racket like a goddess. Now in her early thirties, there is no question that Aretha has "arrived."

But it was not always this way for her. When she is asked about the electrifying quality in her singing, Aretha explains: "I guess most people call it 'soul.' This is something I got from growing up in my father's church, singing with him and hearing his sermons every Sunday.

7

You hear him preach just one sermon, and you'll know that he's a past master of 'soul'.''

Many people perhaps are not that familiar with Aretha's early life. They know her as the girl who has won two gold records, ($1,000,000 worth of records at wholesale or about 500,000 copies), or as the girl who earns more than one-half million dollars a year from records and concert work, or as the singer who receives more TV and concert offers than she can accept.

But actually the fame came slowly. Aretha was born in Memphis, Tennessee, on March 25, 1942. When she was two years old, her family moved first to Buffalo, and then five years later to Detroit. Her father was the Reverend C.L. Franklin, a minister and a gospel singer himself. Indeed he has been the pastor of the New Bethel Baptist Church in Detroit for the last 20 years.

There were five children in the family, three girls and two boys. The family was always pretty well off, ''always had enough of everything.'' Aretha recalls only one hardship, the death of her mother who died when Aretha was ten years old. It was hard on the family then because their father was often away for a month at a time. (He would tour the South conducting revival meetings.)

While their father was gone, the girls took care of the house and went to school during the week. Aretha also sang in the choir twice a week. Sometimes she would join her father on the weekend, singing on his revival tour.

With her father, she met some of the great gospel singers — Sam Cooke, Mahalia Jackson, and Clara Ward. Not only did she meet them, she listened to their music and learned from them.

Of that experience, Aretha has said, ''I learned a lot,

especially from Sam Cooke," always one of her favorite singers. "He did so many things with his voice — so gentle one minute, so swinging the next, then electrifying, always doing something else." She was deeply affected by his death in 1964.

Clara Ward also influenced her. "Clara knocked me out. From then on, I knew I wanted to sing." She knew that at ten when she was in her father's church choir. She also knew that she would need to be able to play the piano so that she could accompany herself, so she began trying to teach herself to play. She listened to Eddie Heywood records, "just playin', but finding a little somethin' here and there."

Her father finally hired a piano teacher, but Aretha didn't like the way she taught her. "When she'd come, I'd hide. I just couldn't take it. She had the baby piano books, and I wanted to go directly to the tunes." But Aretha continued to play and sing on her own. This was natural in her father's house.

B.B. King, Arthur Prysock, Dorothy Donegan and Dinah Washington often stayed with her father. She met Lou Rawls, James Cleveland, and Art Tatum. Tatum really impressed Aretha with "the way he could just sit down and play. I just cancelled that out for me and knew that I could never do that, but he left a strong impression on me, as a pianist and a person."

Above all others, Aretha said, her father had the greatest impact on her. The way her father brought his preaching and his music together really impressed Aretha. As she herself puts it, "Most of what I learned vocally came from him. He gave me a sense of timing in music and timing is important in everything."

When she was thirteen, Aretha made two single

records, *Never Grow Old,* and *Precious Lord, Take My Hand.* They were gospel songs, and they established her reputation as a young singer. But at that time, she still did not think she would become a performer.

That changed in 1960. She was 18 years old then. Major 'Mule' Holly, the bassist for the jazz pianist, Teddy Wilson, told her she could be a popular singer. He said that she had a certain basic style that was salable in jazz or popular music.

Aretha's father decided to help her in this effort. So they came to New York City together to make demonstration records of her voice. By playing these "demos," she could show people that she could really sing. They could hear her on a record before they met her in person — if they wanted to.

At the same time, Aretha went to a special school which helped to train her as a performer. She continued to study music as well. One day a man by the name of John Hammond at Columbia Records heard one of Aretha's "demos." He liked what he heard. He thought that Aretha had a real singing talent. After he invited her in to sing for him, Hammond decided to sign Aretha for a five-year contract with Columbia Records.

In many ways, this was a big break for Aretha. Now she was able to get night club dates and concerts. She could also make records for Columbia. Those records sold, but Aretha never made a best-selling record. She was doing well, but she was not at the top of her profession.

Part of this had to do with Aretha. She got into all kinds of trouble with agents and managers. They thought she was too emotional. She played nightclubs but not too successfully. She herself later said, "I was afraid. I

sang to the floor a lot." Part of the problem had to do with Columbia Records. Hammond had thought that Aretha would sing her own music. Columbia tried to turn Aretha into a pop music star. Black rhythm-and-blues singers had only limited success in the "pop" market. "Black music" was still considered a thing apart, special and different.

In music catalogues, black music was listed under "race," "ebony," or "sepia." This said that the performer was black and that the record had been made for a black audience. White musicians would often "borrow" black music and make recordings of their own. These were called "covering records." They were widely distributed and made money, but no money was paid to the black composer who wrote the music or the black musician who performed it.

Aretha Franklin, therefore, had a foot in both worlds, and this fact was a problem for her. Her heritage and background were black. Her record company was white. When Aretha finally left Columbia Records in 1966, it was a different world. The interest in folk-rock music created a great interest in "rhythm and blues" — black music.

Thus when Martha and the Vandellas sang, "Calling out around the world! Are you ready for a brand new beat?" black people knew that beat went back to their roots — back to gospel singing, jazz, Bessie Smith, Art Tatum, Billie Holiday — back to who they were.

And then Aretha came. After she left Columbia Records, she signed up with Atlantic. In two weeks, her first record sold one-quarter of a million copies. Her voice had a powerful driving energy that just flowed from her. Behind her was the gospel beat. Mahalia Jackson had called gospel "a powerful beat, a rhythm we held on to

from slavery days." That beat had been injected with anger and pride. Aretha's music celebrated that beat.

The man who had seen all of this was Jerry Wexler, a vice-president at Atlantic Records. He sees Aretha this way: "I'd say she's a musical genius comparable to that other great musical genius, Ray Charles. Both play a terrific gospel piano which is one of the greatest assets one can have today. Since they have this broader talent, they can bring to a recording session a total conception of the music, and thus contribute much more than the average artist."

When Aretha goes to a recording session, she has already made a "lead arrangement." She has often written the music herself. She knows the sound she wants. Often the "group" that sings along or "backs" Aretha is made up of her and her sisters, Erma and Carolyn. Their voices are dubbed in later.

The "soul sound" she creates is simply a sound for all people. "Everybody who's living has problems and desires just as I do. When the fellow on the corner has somethin' botherin' him, he feels the same way I do. When we cry, we all gonna cry tears; and when we laugh, we all have to smile."

After a concert tour, Aretha enjoys just being alone. "When I'm not workin', I like to come in the house and sit down and be very quiet. Sometimes nobody even knows I'm home. I don't care too much about goin' out. By the time I get home, I've had enough of nightclubs."

Aretha and her manager-husband Ted White, have bought a home in Detroit where they spend as much time as they can. There, with her husband and her four sons, she has "a lot of family fun."

Aretha also owns an apartment in New York City

where she sometimes stops off to rest. She enjoys these homes because she can be herself. "I must do what is real in me in all ways. It might bug some and offend others; but this is what I must live by, the truth, so long as it doesn't impose on others."

Aretha is still a very shy person. Before she is to go on in a nightclub, for example, she becomes very nervous. One way she has learned to overcome this nervousness is to pretend that she is "just at a party, and the audience is just my friends." As she sings, she loses herself in her music. Then she is no longer afraid or nervous. She belts out her songs over a pounding rhythm-and-blues beat. As she sings, she is caught up in the emotion. She will shout in the middle of a song, "Yeah! I believe it!"

It took years for Aretha to feel that naturalness before a large audience. As she puts it: "What has happened is that over the years I've gained enough experience to work anywhere and to relate to people on all levels. I know I've improved my overall look and sound; they're much better. And I've gained a great deal of confidence in myself. I wonder how many people know I once had this big problem about actually walking out on the stage.

"Sometimes I still have that problem . . . You know, it's a thing about whether everything is hanging right, whether my hair looks O.K. . . . . all those people sitting out there looking at me, checking me out from head to toe. Wow! That really used to get to me; but I've overcome most of that by just walking out on the stage night after night, year after year."

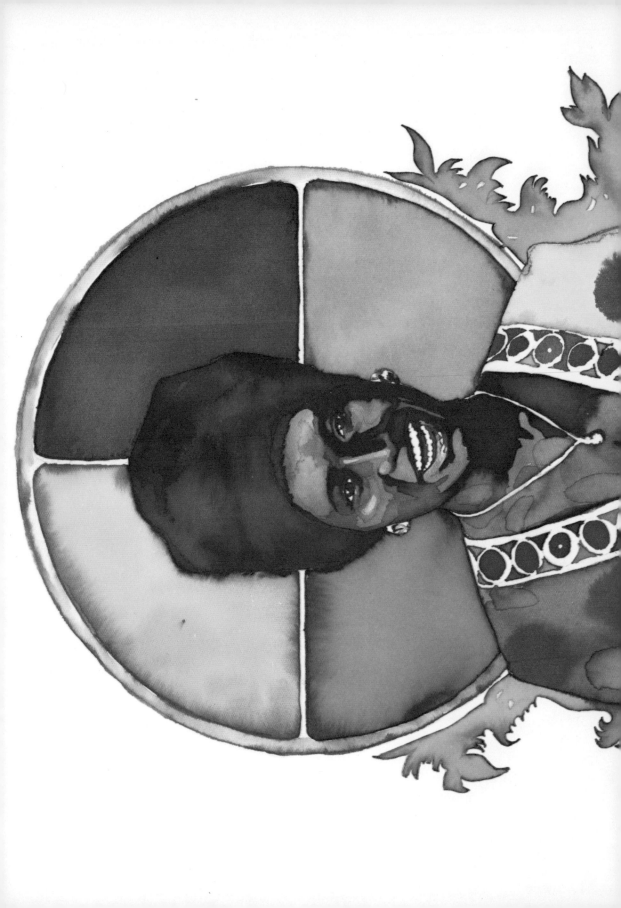

When she is asked how she could have such fears after a childhood of singing in church and before large crowds, she answers: "I don't know whether you can call them real fears, or that they just all come from the fact that I had no confidence in my natural self. I suppose I wanted to look a lot more glamorous, you know, so I came off looking very starched.

"At the root of it was the thing I had for years about wanting to be a little shorter, so I tried to shorten myself by sort of stooping over when I walked. That developed improper posture, which is something I really had to work on. Well, I worked on it, and now I walk tall, and I'm proud of myself just as I am."

Along with performing, composing is also a very important part of Aretha's life. The songs she writes usually have a very special meaning for her. They are *personal* expressions. "Well, it's true that I really have to *feel* a song before I'll deal with it, and just about every song I do is based either on an experience I've had or an experience that someone I know has gone through."

She had these things to say about her song, *Brand New Me*: "That's one that expresses exactly how I felt when I recorded it, and actually how I feel right now — like a brand new woman, a brand new me. I'm feeling much brighter these days; I'm a far gayer person. Like, I'm coming up with a lot of fresh, new material; and I'm putting a lot more into working on my act. Well, it's just that I've gotten rid of a lot of things that were weighting me down; and I'm, well . . . like a new person right now."

Aretha has also started her own talent company, ALF Productions. ALF has a number of musical performers under contract — Albertina Walker and the Caravans, Almeta Lattimer, Saman and Billy Always. Aretha and her

sister, Carolyn, have started their own record label "Do It To It." Finally, she has her musical tours which take her all over the United States. She performs in nightclubs; she sings in prisons. She even goes out of the United States to places like the Virgin Islands and Africa.

Aretha puts her social concerns into her work. About Africa, she says, "I made them give me a contract in which I specify that I won't sing before any segregated audiences. They'll either be totally integrated or all-black. I won't sing for an all-white audience. Black people must be able to come and hear me sing."

Now in her early thirties, Aretha is certainly "getting it together." She has been a performer since childhood, she was a professional singer in her teens, she was successful at Columbia Records, and she has been a superstar for the last six years.

Aretha is certainly not glamorous. Unlike Diana Ross or Dionne Warwick, Aretha does not have a beautiful face and figure. She is very quiet, and, some say, still shy. Nonetheless, she is certainly the ranking black singer of the 70's. Since 1967, she has won nearly all the available prizes including five Grammy Awards and two Female Singer-of-the-Year designations.

She is a millionaire many times over, and her income is over one-half million dollars a year. She has it all, and so she says: "It's all been wonderful, like a giant, happy dream. I always knew I could sing, but I never suspected it would be anything at all like this."

Aretha's greatest joy, however, is in concert. There her fourteen years of trial and experience come together. Her singing and piano playing work together electrically. At a recent concert, she was finishing by going into a "yeah" saying call. The audience came back with, "yeah!"

Then she started singing her song *Spirit in the Dark*. That song says that, when you are feeling bad, you should cover your eyes with one hand. Put your other hand on your hip. Next the song continues, wait until the spirit in the dark comes pounding inside you. When you finally feel it, you'll be feeling good again.

Aretha finished the song to the roaring applause of the audience. Then she walked off the stage. A few seconds later she came back on the stage. She had Ray Charles on her arm. She led the blind pianist to the microphone. She sat down at the piano, and the two of them continued the song.

Ray Charles beamed. The whole crowd went along with them. Ray and Aretha traded shouts, breaks, jumps and howls. The crowd danced, clapped, hugged, kissed and cried. People ran down to the stage and tried to touch her. Aretha now got Ray to play the piano while she took his place at the microphone. And play he did to dazzling perfection. Finally, his face covered with sweat, Ray left the stage. Aretha stepped forward to the front of the stage to close the show.

She looked at the audience. Everyone was quiet. She sang a soft song. It was about reaching out a hand to a friend and "making this a better world if you can." With the song finished, she faced the audience and bowed. She turned to each side of the audience and bowed deeply. She spoke her thanks to the band. She spoke her thanks to the crowd. Then she said goodbye to everyone. "I love you. I love you all, " she said.

She walked off the stage; she was gone. The stage was completely empty, the lights went up, and the crowd started to file out of the auditorium.

Aretha Speaks

"I must do what is real in me in all ways. It might bug some and offend others, but this is what I must live by, the truth, so long as it doesn't impose on others."

"Respect. If you can get that, you can get the rest of it. Without it, you can't put anything together."

"Life's a whole lot like pinochle [a card game]. It's all in your hand. You got nothin' to start with, and what you can get is up to how well you can play the game."

"A woman's place should be where she's most comfortable, but it should also be behind her man first, her children second, and then herself. Men are men, and women are women, and a woman shouldn't be afraid to be feminine."

"It's all been wonderful, like a giant happy dream. I always knew I could sing, but I never suspected it would be anything at all like this."

"White kids appreciate soul. The college kids where I perform want honesty in their music, and that's what soul is all about."

"I like life. And I love people. You'll never find me messing with drugs. Life is just too beautiful."

"Well, I believe that the Black Revolution certainly forced me and the majority of black people to begin taking a second look at ourselves. It wasn't that we were all that ashamed of ourselves; we merely started appreciating our *natural* selves . . . sort of, you know, falling in love with ourselves *just as we are*. We found that we had far more to be proud of."

JACKSON FIVE
CARLY SIMON
BOB DYLAN
JOHN DENVER
THE BEATLES
ELVIS PRESLEY
JOHNNY CASH
CHARLEY PRIDE
ARETHA FRANKLIN
ROBERTA FLACK
STEVIE WONDER

Rock'n
PopStars